Jesus Our Life

Activity Book

Jesus Our Life

Activity Book

Faith and Life Series

Third Edition

BOOK TWO

Ignatius Press, San Francisco
Catholics United for the Faith, Steubenville, Ohio

Director of First Edition: The late Rev. Msgr. Eugene Kevane, Ph.D.
Assistant Director and General Editor of First Edition: Patricia I. Puccetti, M.A.
First Edition Writer: Barbara M. Nacelewicz
First Edition Artist: Gary Hoff; David Previtali

Revision Writer: Colette Ellis, M.A.
Revision Editor: Christopher A. Bess
Revision Artist: Christopher J. Pelicano

Catholics United for the Faith, Inc. and Ignatius Press gratefully acknowledge the guidance and assistance of the late Reverend Monsignor Eugene Kevane, former Director of the Pontifical Catechetical Institute, Diocese of Arlington, Virginia, in the production of the First Edition of this series. This First Edition intended to implement the authentic approach in Catholic catechesis given to the Church through documents of the Holy See and in particular the Conference of Joseph Cardinal Ratzinger on "Sources and Transmission of Faith." The Revised Edition and Third Edition continue this commitment by drawing upon the *Catechism of the Catholic Church* (Libreria Editrice Vaticana, © 1994, 1997).

2017 reprint
See www.faithandlifeseries.com
for additional tools and resources

ISBN 978-1-58617-572-6
Manufactured by Friesens Corporation
Manufactured in Altona, MB, Canada, in March 2017
Job # 230676
in compliance with the
Consumer Protection Safety Act

Contents

Dear Student,

This year you will read and learn about God and His love for us. Your teacher will help you to understand what you have read about Creation, God's love, God's Laws, Jesus the Savior, the Sacraments, and the Catholic Church.

This *Faith and Life* activity book is one of the many ways you can think about and remember what you have learned. With this book you will draw and color pictures, work on different puzzles, and memorize many of the truths you learned in class. Be sure to ask your teacher or parents any questions you might have.

As you prepare to receive the Sacraments, this book can help you grow closer to Jesus Christ and His Church.

Name:______________________

I Am a Child of God!

**"How precious is your mercy,
O God!"** Psalm 36:7

Draw a picture of yourself and God the Father.

Name:____________________

Look up these words in the back of your book and write their meanings.

Heaven: ______________________________________

Soul: ______________________________________

Can you answer these questions?

1. Who made you?

____

2. Who is God?

____

3. Where is God?

____

4. Does God know everything?

____

Name:____________________

God Is Everywhere

List some places where God is.

1. ______________________________

2. ______________________________

3. ______________________________

Draw a picture of one of these places.

Name:____________________

Bible Facts

Answer the following questions.

Who gave us the Bible?

____

What is the Bible?

____

What does the Bible tell us about?

____

Who wrote the Bible?

____

The Bible has two parts. What are they?

1.____________________________________

2.____________________________________

Name:____________________

Draw a picture of yourself with God in your heart.

Name:____________________

The Blessed Trinity

One God in Three Persons

Color the circle with "The Father" red, "The Son" blue, and "The Holy Spirit" yellow. Then color the sections with the word "is" orange, and the sections with "is not" black.

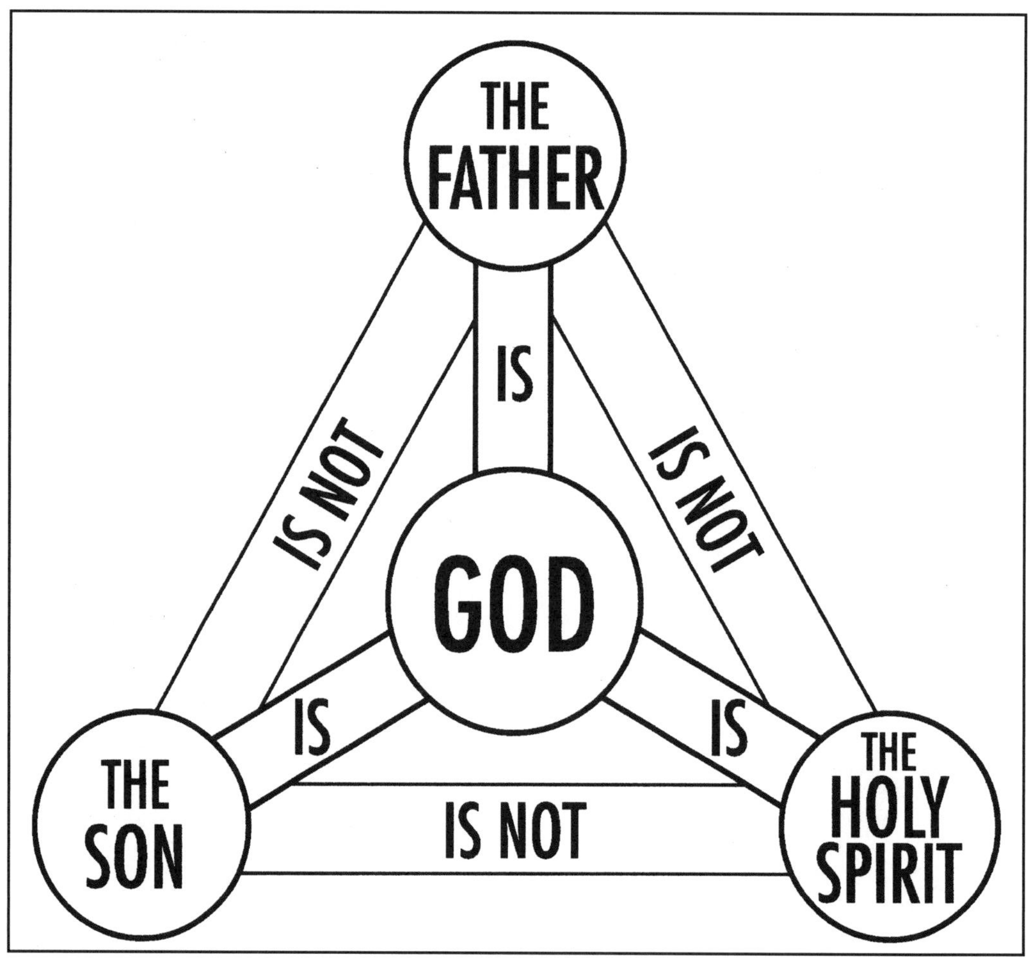

Name:____________________

The Blessed Trinity

Use the following words to help you fill in the blanks.

One	Father	always	died
God	Son	Jesus	rose
three	Holy Spirit	Heaven	cowboy
Person	earth	Savior	four

There is only _ _ _ God, but in _ _ _ there are _ _ _ _ _ Persons. The three Persons are equal and _ _ _ _ _ _ were. The _ _ _ _ _ _ is the First Person. He created Heaven and _ _ _ _ _ . The _ _ _ is the Second _ _ _ _ _ _ . His name is _ _ _ _ _ . He came down from _ _ _ _ _ _ to be our _ _ _ _ _ _ . Jesus _ _ _ _ for us and _ _ _ _ from the dead. The _ _ _ _ _ _ _ _ _ _ is the Third Person of the Blessed Trinity.

Name:____________________

Word Search

Can you find these words in the puzzle?
Look carefully! The words go across and down.

BODY	CHRIST	MASS
HEAVEN	HOLY SPIRIT	ONE
JESUS	GREAT	SON
SOUL	BIBLE	GOOD
CROSS	OLD	HOLY

```
B O D Y A E N C R O S S R
E L S T E S X G E Y K Z A
H D K H A U I D A Y L E N
K H E A V E N K S O N N T
G O O D L R I A T D H N S
K N T T E R E K E M T A O
V E G M I M A S S I E A U
H O L Y L U E S U S T L L
B I B L E S V E G R E A T
B G R K S C H R I S T I S
A L L E J E S U S L P T T
T H O H O L Y S P I R I T
```

Name:____________________

The Order of Creation

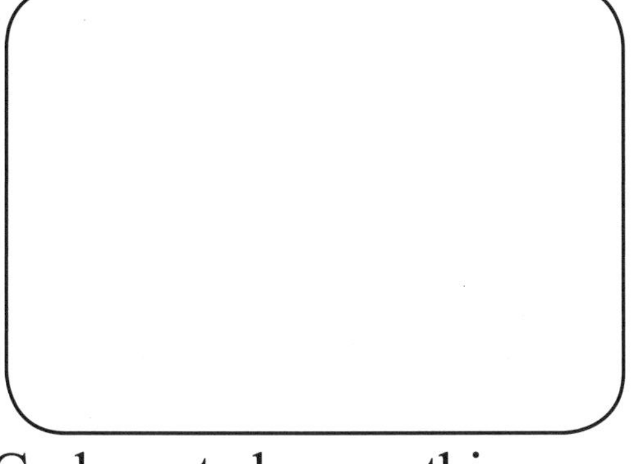

God created many things that do not have life in them. In the box above, draw something God created that does not have life.

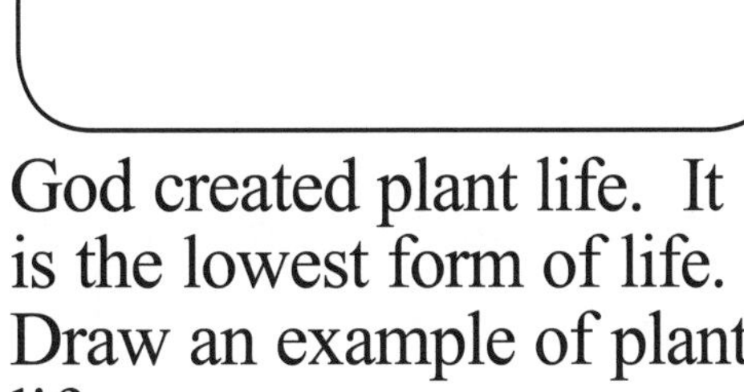

God created plant life. It is the lowest form of life. Draw an example of plant life.

God created animal life. It is above plant life, but below human life. Animals can move and grow. They can also be trained. Draw an example of animal life.

Human life is the highest form of life. We can grow and move like the animals, but we can also think and act freely. Draw a picture of yourself.

Name:____________________

God Is the Creator!

1. Why did God make Heaven and earth?

2. How did God make things?

3. By looking at the sky, the ocean, or a mountain, we see that they are mighty and powerful. What can they teach us about God?

4. How can we praise and thank God for His gifts?

5. Does God take care of all His creation?

6. Does God take care of you?

Name:____________________

Write a letter to God thanking Him for His gift of creation.

Dear God,

____

____

____

____

____

Love,

____

This page intentionally left blank.

Name:____________________

Word Search

Can you find these words in the puzzle?
Look carefully! The words go across and down.

EVE	ANIMALS	NEIGHBOR
CHILDREN	GOD	GARDEN OF EDEN
GUARDIAN	FATHER	GRACE
HEAVEN	LOVE	KNOW
LIFE	PRAYER	NAMES
PEOPLE	ANGEL	SERVE

L	X	C	H	I	L	D	R	E	N	X	E
X	E	V	E	H	J	A	N	G	E	L	A
G	A	R	D	E	N	O	F	E	D	E	N
O	D	L	X	L	S	G	R	A	C	E	I
D	A	O	X	P	U	X	X	P	R	A	M
A	M	V	X	X	P	R	A	Y	E	R	A
C	P	E	O	P	L	E	X	X	F	X	L
H	X	H	E	A	V	E	N	S	A	X	S
X	E	N	A	M	E	S	N	E	T	L	R
K	N	O	W	T	L	E	S	R	H	I	E
N	E	I	G	H	B	O	R	V	E	F	X
G	U	A	R	D	I	A	N	E	R	E	X

Name:____________________

God's Children

As God's children, we are called to know, love, and serve God. How can we know God? Unscramble the words below to find out.

1. DARE HET LIBBE: ________ _____ ________

2. RPAY: ___________

3. ERLNA YROU GELRINOI: ___________ _____

____

4. OG TO SASM: _____ _____ __________

5. LAKT OT ROUY RAPETNS ____________ _____

_________ _________________

pray	Commandments	learn
neighbor	everyone	worship

We are to love God. How can we do this? Fill in the blanks with the words above to find out.

6. To love God, I can keep His _________________.
I can _________ to Him and tell Him I love Him. I can love my ________________ , who is ______________.
I can ___________ about God and ______________ Him.

Name:____________________

Angel of God, my guardian dear,
To whom God's love commits me here,
Ever this day, be at my side,
To light and guard, to rule and guide. *Amen.*

This week, before getting dressed, pray the Guardian Angel Prayer. Put a check in the box each day you pray to your guardian angel.

Monday	Tuesday	Wednesday	Thursday	Friday	Saturday	Sunday

Name:____________________

Saint Michael, the Archangel, defend us in battle; be our protection against the wickedness and snares of the devil; may God rebuke him, we humbly pray, and do thou, O Prince of the Heavenly host, by the power of God, cast into Hell Satan and all the evil spirits who wander about the world seeking the ruin of souls. *Amen.*

This week, before bed, pray the Saint Michael Prayer. Put a check in the box each day you pray.

Monday	Tuesday	Wednesday	Thursday	Friday	Saturday	Sunday

Name:____________________

Word Search

Can you find these words in the puzzle?
Look carefully! The words go across and down.

ANGELS	HELL
DEVIL	HELPER
EARTH	SMARTER
GOD	SPIRITS
HEAVEN	THINK

X	S	S	M	A	R	T	E	R	S
H	B	I	R	T	H	D	A	Y	A
E	J	X	H	E	A	V	E	N	V
L	O	B	E	Y	D	X	X	X	T
L	S	X	L	X	E	A	R	T	H
H	E	L	P	E	V	H	E	M	I
X	P	X	E	A	I	Y	X	X	N
X	H	X	R	X	L	X	X	X	K
S	P	I	R	I	T	S	G	O	D
A	N	G	E	L	S	G	E	R	X

Name:____________________

We can be good or bad through words, actions, and even through things we don't do at all.

Circle your answers to these questions.

1. You ask your Mother if you may go out and play with a friend. She says No. Do you go and ask your Father? YES NO

2. Someone in your class forgot his lunch. Do you share yours? YES NO

3. Your brother or sister has been bothering you all week. You receive two cookies. Do you share them with him or her? YES NO

4. You break a rule at home. Do you lie about it? YES NO

5. A friend has hurt your feelings. Do you call him a bad name? YES NO

Name:____________________

Fill in the blanks.

Before Original Sin	After Original Sin
1. Adam and Eve were happy in the Garden of Eden.	1.
2.	2. The animals were afraid of Adam and Eve.
3. Adam and Eve were never sick or hurt. They did not suffer.	3.
4. God told Adam and Eve all that they needed to know.	4.
5.	5. Adam and Eve no longer had grace in their souls.
6. God would talk to Adam and Eve in the garden.	6.
7.	7. Adam and Eve would die.
8. Adam and Eve did not have to work hard for food.	8.
9.	9. God was offended by their Original Sin.
10.	10. Adam and Eve could not go to Heaven

Name:____________________

Can you fill in the blanks? Use chapters four, five, and six for help.

God loved __________ and _______ very much. He gave them a special gift called ______________ .

Grace is a share in _______'s own life. With grace in their souls, Adam and Eve became God's children. Because of grace, Adam and Eve would someday be able to live with God in Heaven. Today, God offers us the same gift He gave _______ and ______ . We receive God's ________ in the Sacrament of Baptism. God wants us to be His __________________ and to be happy with Him in Heaven.

Name:____________________

Baptism

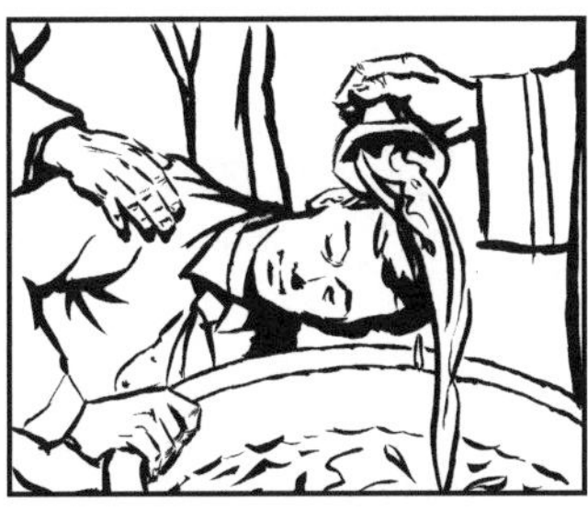

grace	souls	Heaven	God
Original	first	Adam	Baptism
Sin	Eve	washed	

Fill in the blanks with the words above.

When ___________ and Eve sinned, they lost the gift of God's grace in their souls. They could not get to ___________. Their children were born with Original Sin, too. They had no grace in their souls.

We call Adam and Eve our ___________ parents because all people came from them. So did you. And we were all born with __________ ______ on our souls.

At ______________, Original Sin was __________ away, and your soul was filled with God's life of grace. Now you are able to go to Heaven and be with _______.

Name:____________________

Can you answer these questions?

1. What are angels?

2. What is sin?

3. Who committed the first sin on earth?

4. What is this first sin called?

5. What is Baptism?

6. What did Baptism do for you?

Name:____________________

It is very important to try our best to keep our souls as clean as the day we were baptized. What are some things we can do to keep our souls holy and pleasing to God?

____

____

____

____

____

____

____

____

Name:______________________

Draw a picture of your patron saint or your favorite saint.

Name:____________________

Draw Adam and Eve 1	Draw Noah and his ark 2
Draw Abraham and Isaac 3	Draw David and Goliath 4

Name:____________________

Word Search

Can you find these words in the puzzle?
Look carefully! The words go across and down.

ABRAHAM	FAMILY	OBEDIENT
ARK	JOSEPH	TESTED
EVE	DAVID	ANGEL
MARY	ANIMALS	GOD
ADAM	CHILDREN	ISAAC
BAPTISM	HEAVEN	LOVE
	SAVIOR	

O	X	A	B	R	A	H	A	M	N	X	E
B	S	R	A	N	N	A	N	G	L	L	V
E	A	K	P	O	G	O	G	H	D	O	E
D	V	L	T	E	S	T	E	D	C	C	S
I	I	G	I	H	U	X	L	P	R	H	J
E	O	O	S	J	O	S	E	P	H	I	O
N	R	D	M	I	S	A	A	C	F	L	R
T	X	H	E	A	V	E	N	D	A	D	F
L	O	V	E	M	A	R	Y	A	D	R	P
F	A	M	I	L	Y	E	S	V	A	E	H
A	N	I	M	A	L	S	R	I	M	N	X
B	P	I	S	R	O	X	N	D	R	E	X

Name: ____________________

Can you match the person with the event?

Person	Event
ADAM	Was his old father's only son.
EVE	Wanted to fight.
NOAH	Named the animals.
ABRAHAM	Built an ark.
ISAAC	Was sad because he did not have children.
GOLIATH	Was tricked by a snake.

Questions from your text.

1. Why were the people waiting? When did they start waiting?

2. What happened when the people were waiting?

3. Why did people laugh at Noah?

4. Why did Abraham agree to give up his son Isaac? In the end did he have to give him up?

This page intentionally left blank.

Name:____________________

Color the picture

With the help of your textbook, fill in these blanks.

God gave the Chosen People a _____________. His name was ___________. With God's help, ___________ set the people ___________. For many years God led the people so they could find a new _________ to live in. God wanted His Chosen _____________ really to know that they were special to Him. He took __________ of them and showed His ________ for them by __________ __________ ________ ___________ _____________ God also wanted them to ___________ __________ in return. He gave His Chosen People ___________ and told them that if they loved Him they would __________ those rules and they would be_____________.

Name:____________________

Write the Ten Commandments under the Great Commandments into which they fit.

Love the Lord your God with all your heart, with all your soul, with all your strength, and all your mind.

1.______________________________

2.______________________________

3.______________________________

Love your neighbor as yourself.

4.______________________________

5.______________________________

6.______________________________

7.______________________________

8.______________________________

9.______________________________

10.______________________________

Name:____________________

Write in your own words what each Commandment says.

COMMANDMENT

1st Commandment: ______________________________

2nd Commandment: ______________________________

3rd Commandment: ______________________________

4th Commandment: ______________________________

5th Commandment: ______________________________

6th Commandment: ______________________________

7th Commandment: ______________________________

8th Commandment: ______________________________

9th Commandment: ______________________________

10th Commandment: ______________________________

This page intentionally left blank.

Name:_____________________

Unscramble the Ten Commandments. Write them properly below the scrambled words. Put them in order by number.

_____ HRONO YROU RHAFTE NDA THOMRE.

____

_____ UOY LAHSL ONT VAHE HTOER GDOS DESBIES EM.

____

_____ YUO LLASH TNO IEL.

____

_____ OYU HALSL ONT VETOC OURY EIGHNOBS'R FIWE.

____

_____ BMEMERER OT EEKP GD'SO YDA OLYH.

____

_____ UYO LLSHA TNO LKIL.

____

_____ OUY LSAHL NTO LTSEA.

____

_____ OYU LSLHA ONT VCETO UORY EIGHNS'BRO ODOGS.

____

_____ OUY HSLAL TON SEU D'SOG MNAE NI VIAN.

____

_____ UOY LLSHA OTN MIMOCT DYUALTRE.

____

Name:____________________

Prayer is our way of talking with God and listening to Him. It keeps us in a relationship with God. It is our way of talking to God and listening to Him. We can pray out loud or in our hearts. There are different ways to pray. We can adore and love God. We can thank God for His gifts. We can ask God for the things we need. We can pray for other people. Can you think of some things to pray to God about?

ADORATION PRAYER—LOVING GOD

For example: I love You God because you are all good.

____

____

THANKING GOD

For example: I thank You God for giving me a good day.

____

____

ASKING GOD FOR THINGS WE NEED

For example: God, I need to learn more about You. Can You help me?

____

____

PRAYING FOR OTHER PEOPLE

For example: Lord, my friend is sick. Can You help my friend get better?

____

Name:____________________

List Ways We Love God	List Ways We Love Our Neighbors

Name:____________________

Sin

With the help of your textbook, fill in these blanks.

God gave you the power to choose to _______ Him. You can choose to do what you know is right or what you know is ______. When you do wrong, it isn't because you "________ to." No one makes you do it. Only ______ can choose. At times it is hard to be _______, but that is when you can ________ God that you really __________ Him.

If we do something bad on purpose, we commit a ______. We do not love God when we sin. With each sin we turn away from _______. It is not a sin if we _______ to do something. But if we are ___________ to do something wrong, and we __________, "Yes I will do it, even though I know it's wrong," then we commit a ________, and turn away from God.

Name:______________________

The Savior

1. Why did God send a Savior?

2. Who was the Savior?

3. How did God prepare the people for the Savior?

4. How do we get ready for the Savior?

Name:____________________

Answer the following questions.

1. Who did God choose to be the Mother of the Savior?

2. Was Mary born with Original Sin?

3. What was Mary's soul like?

4. Was Mary pleasing to God? Why?

5. What angel came to ask Mary to be the Mother of the Savior?

Name: ______________________

The Annunciation

Color the picture.

This page intentionally left blank.

Name:____________________

Review Questions

1. Who is the Mother of Jesus?

2. Was anyone besides Jesus ever free from Original Sin?

3. Where was Jesus born?

4. When was Jesus born?

5. Who is Jesus Christ?

6. Why did the Son of God become man?

Name:____________________

Pretend you are Mary or Joseph. What would you have written in your diary when Jesus was born?

Name:______________________

Joy in Receiving Jesus

We receive Jesus at Christmas.

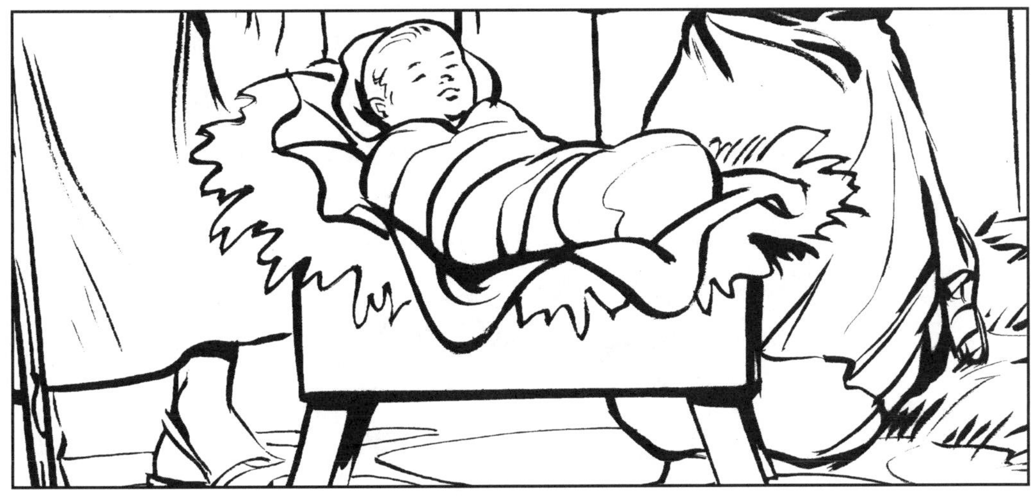

We receive Jesus in Holy Communion.

Name:______________________

God knew how important families are. He sent His only begotten Son into the world to live in a family with Mary and Joseph. He gave you a family, with your mother and father. Through your Baptism, you are also part of God's family with Mary as your Mother, God as your Father, and Jesus as your brother! This Christmas, pray for families.

Name:______________________

Saint Joseph

1. Who is Saint Joseph?

2. What did he do?

3. What are some words that tell us about Saint Joseph?

Name:____________________

Blessed Mother

1. Who is the Blessed Virgin Mary?

2. What did Mary do in the Holy Family?

3. What are some words that tell us about Mary?

Name: ____________________

The Child Jesus

1. What do we know about Jesus?

2. What did the Holy Family do together?

Name:____________________

Word Search

Can you find these words in the puzzle?
Look carefully! The words go across and down.

ANGEL	CLOTHES	HOLY
ANIMALS	EGYPT	FAMILY
BABY	FATHER	POOR
BETHLEHEM	FOOD	PROTECTS
CARPENTER	FRIENDS	SAVIOR
CHRISTMAS	GAMES	SHEPHERD
CLEAN	HEROD	STAR

S	C	S	H	E	P	H	E	R	D	P	E
X	L	V	C	L	O	T	H	E	S	R	A
B	E	T	H	L	E	H	E	M	I	O	N
A	A	H	R	E	S	O	F	E	S	T	I
K	N	E	I	P	F	L	A	G	E	E	M
E	S	R	S	O	O	Y	M	Y	E	C	A
D	T	O	T	O	O	E	I	P	F	T	L
A	A	D	M	R	D	E	L	T	A	S	S
N	R	G	A	M	E	S	Y	E	T	L	B
G	N	O	S	A	V	I	O	R	H	I	A
E	F	R	I	E	N	D	S	V	E	F	B
L	C	A	R	P	E	N	T	E	R	E	Y

Name: ______________________

Color the picture of Jesus' Baptism.

Draw a picture of the Temptation in the Desert.

Name:____________________

Jesus picked twelve men to be His disciples. They would be His special helpers and each would spread His Word like mustard seeds throughout the world. The disciples soon learned from Jesus how to preach the Good News. Find in your Bible (Matthew 10:1–4) the names of the disciples and write them under the picture below.

1.____________	5.____________	9.____________
2.____________	6.____________	10.____________
3.____________	7.____________	11.____________
4.____________	8.____________	12.____________

Name:____________________

Jesus taught us about the Kingdom in parables. Draw a picture of one of the parables about the Kingdom.

The Kingdom is like ____________________________
because ________________________________

____

Name:____________________

Good News Is Preached!

Who?

What?

Where?

Why?

When?

Draw a picture for your article.

Tell me about the Kingdom of God.

Who is the King of this Kingdom?

Who is invited to live there?

Name:____________________

Answer the following questions.

1. What did the third man do for the man who was robbed?

2. Did the third man love Jesus in this man?

3. What does it mean to love God in our neighbor?

4. How can you be like the third man?

5. List some ways you can love your neighbor.

Name:____________________

Word Search

Can you find these words in the puzzle?
Look carefully! The words go across and down.

FEED	DEAD	IMPRISONED
HUNGRY	HELP	LOVE GOD
CLOTHE	GIVE DRINK	LOVE OTHERS
NAKED	THIRSTY	BE KIND
VISIT THE SICK	SHELTER	BURY
	HOMELESS	

V	I	S	I	T	T	H	E	S	I	C	K
L	G	I	V	E	D	R	I	N	K	F	B
O	B	U	R	Y	I	D	E	A	D	E	E
V	D	L	X	E	N	O	F	E	D	E	K
E	I	M	P	R	I	S	O	N	E	D	I
G	M	V	X	P	U	X	X	P	R	T	N
O	N	A	K	E	D	R	A	Y	E	H	D
D	X	H	U	N	G	R	Y	X	F	I	S
H	O	M	E	L	E	S	S	S	A	R	R
E	N	C	L	O	T	H	E	E	T	S	E
L	O	V	E	O	T	H	E	R	S	T	X
P	S	H	E	L	T	E	R	V	E	Y	X

Name:____________________

Corporal Works of Mercy	How Can You Live These Works?
1. Feed the hungry.	
2. Give drink to the thristy.	
3. Clothe the naked.	
4. Shelter the homeless.	
5. Visit the sick.	
6. Visit the imprisoned.	
7. Bury the dead.	

This page intentionally left blank.

Name:______________________

Jesus, Teach Me How to Pray.

Color the picture.

Name:____________________

Prayer

Answer the following questions.

1. What is prayer?

2. What did the disciples know they were doing when they were praying?

3. Whom did the disciples ask to teach them how to pray?

4. What prayer did He teach them?

5. For what does this prayer teach us to pray? There are seven things. Can you list them and explain them?

1.
2.
3.
4.
5.
6.
7.

Name:____________________

Kinds of Prayer

When we pray, we can pray to God out loud or in our hearts. When we pray, we talk with and listen to God. There are different kinds of prayer:

1. Adoring or Praise.
With this kind of prayer, we see God for who He is, and tell Him how much we love Him.

2. Thanksgiving.
With this kind of prayer, we thank God for all the gifts He has given to us, such as family, food, and love.

3. Petition.
This means to "ask for." With this kind of prayer, we can ask God for all that we need.

4. Intercession.
This means "to ask in place of someone else." With this kind of prayer, we can pray for other people and their needs.

Name:____________________

Prayer Review

Fill in the blanks.

In the Name of the ____________, and of the __________, and of the Holy ________. *Amen.*

Our ________, Who art in _________, _________be Thy ________. Thy ___________come, Thy will be _________ on earth as it is in ____________. Give us this _______ our daily ________ and forgive us our _______________ as we ___________ those who trespass __________ us; and lead us not into _____________, but ___________ us from __________. *Amen.*

Hail _________, full of _________, the ________ is with thee. Blessed art __________ among _________ and blessed is the __________ of thy womb, ____________. Holy Mary, ______ of ______, pray for us ______, now and at the ________ of our __________. *Amen.*

Glory be to the __________, and to the _______, and to the _______ __________. As it was in the ______________, is now, and _______ shall be, world ___________ end. *Amen.*

Name:____________________

Jesus made the lame to walk and the blind to see.

Color the picture.

Name:____________________

Miracles

1. What did Jesus want people to believe?

2. Why did Jesus work miracles?

3. What different miracles did Jesus do?

4. What happened during a storm? Why were the disciples surprised?

Color the picture.

Name:____________________

Write about the miracle that Jesus did with loaves and fish.

Name:____________________

"Little girl, I say to you, arise."

Jesus is God and His power is stronger than death!

Name:____________________

Sin

Fill in the blanks with the words below.

sorry	Laws	loves	sin

Sometimes we break God's ___________. We commit a ________.

Although God hates sins, He ___________ you very much. He is always ready to forgive you when you are ____________ for the sins you committed.

Name:____________________

“Father, I have sinned against Heaven and before you.”

The son had sinned and turned away from the father. When the son was sorry for his sin, he returned to the father, who was very happy to see his son. He forgave his son and embraced him in love and mercy.

Draw the father and son, at the moment the son comes home.

Name:____________________

When we sin, we offend God.
But He wants us to be happy.
He wants us to come back to Him.

Color the picture.

God loves me and lets me choose to do good or bad.
I love God, so I choose to do good!

Name:____________________

1. Do you remember the Ten Commandments?

1.
2.
3.
4.
5.
6.
7.
8.
9.
10.

2. What is sin?

3. What is Mortal Sin?

4. What is Venial Sin?

5. Who forgives sin?

6. Does God love you even if you sin?

7. What should we do if we sin and want to be forgiven?

Name:____________________

Lord Jesus, You cured the sick and forgave sinners. Forgive me and keep me in Your love.

Draw Jesus curing a sick person.

Draw Jesus healing a person with a sick soul because of sin.

Name:____________________

Jesus Forgives

Fill in the blanks with the words below. Some words are used more than once.

God	forgiving	Sacrament	Confession
powers	priests	Penance	today
priest	forgive	through	sins

Only ________ can ________ sins. Jesus showed that He was ___________ by curing people and ____________ their sins. Jesus made some of the disciples His first ____________. He gave them special __________. One of these is the power to _____________ _____. Priests __________have this power too. God forgives our sins ____________ them.

When God uses a _________ to forgive our sins, it is called the ____________ of ______________. It is also called ____________________ because we "confess," or tell our sins to the ______________.

Name:____________________

5 Steps to the Sacrament of Penance:

1. Know what my sins are.
2. Be sorry for my sins.
3. Make up my mind not to sin again.
4. Tell my sins to the priest.
5. Do the penance the priest gives me.

Draw the five steps to Confession.

Name:____________________

In Confession, God forgives my sins and heals my soul! He fills me with His love and mercy and makes me stronger with His grace.

Draw yourself after being forgiven of your sins.

In the picture above…

1. Color the kneeler brown.
2. Circle a Cross in red.
3. Color the priest's hair black.
4. Color the stole purple.

Name:____________________

If you were going on a trip, you would get ready and pack everything you need. You need to get ready for Confession! What kind of things would you "pack" to take with you into the Sacrament of Penance?

Draw lines connecting what you would take with you to Confession to the suitcase.

Accidently spilled cereal

Lied to my mother

Hit my brother

Sneezed at Mass

Forgot to feed the cat

Disobeyed my Father

Cheated on a test

Was very angry about something silly

Stole a candy bar

Destroyed someone's work on purpose

Swallowed bubble gum

Was mean to a boy/girl

Name:____________________

I'm sorry for my sins, O God. Forgive me, a sinner.

Name:____________________

Answer the following questions.

1. What are the five steps to a good Confession?

   1. ______________________________

   2. ______________________________

   3. ______________________________

   4. ______________________________

   5. ______________________________

2. What is a penance?

3. What are the effects of the Sacrament of Penance?

Name:____________________

Word Search

Can you find these words in the puzzle?
Look carefully! The words go across and down.

SACRAMENT	REMEMBER SINS	CONTRITION
HOLY	ABSOLVE	GOOD DEED
FORGIVE	SON	FRIENDSHIP
FATHER	CONFESSIONS	MERCY
PENANCE	SORROW FOR SINS	SIN

R	E	M	E	M	B	E	R	S	I	N	S
C	O	N	T	R	I	T	I	O	N	F	A
O	M	E	R	C	Y	T	E	E	P	R	C
N	E	L	T	E	U	X	L	M	E	I	R
F	O	R	G	I	V	E	S	B	N	E	A
E	C	E	S	U	L	E	X	E	A	N	M
S	F	A	T	H	E	R	N	R	N	D	E
S	I	N	E	A	A	R	Y	A	C	S	N
I	E	H	O	L	Y	S	P	I	E	H	T
O	A	B	S	O	L	V	E	R	M	I	S
N	G	O	O	D	D	E	E	D	X	P	O
S	O	R	R	O	W	F	O	R	S	I	N

Name:____________________

Zacchaeus

Fill in the blanks.

One day, a big crowd of _____________ was with Jesus. A _________________ man named _________________ went up in a _____________ so he could see. Jesus saw him and called out, "______________________________ ____ ____."

Zacchaeus was _______________, but also __________. He knew that his ___________ offended Jesus. So Zacchaeus told Jesus he would _________ ________ for his sins. He paid people ___________ times the money he had taken from them!

Name:____________________

Jesus dies to make up for our sins. We can make up for our sins too!

1. How can you make up for your sins?

2. Why do you do penance?

3. What does our textbook give as examples of penances?

4. Sometimes we have habits of sin. What should we do about this?

Name:____________________

Make a list of penances you can do.

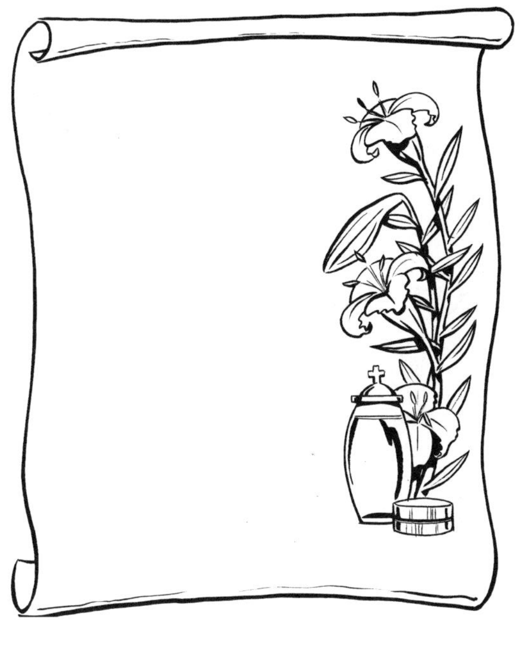

____

____

____

____

____

____

____

Name:______________________

Make sentences with these words.

ABSOLUTION:

____

CONFESSION:

____

FORGIVENESS:

____

PENANCE:

____

SIN:

____

PRIEST:

____

JESUS:

____

Name:____________________

Jesus Christ Is Our King!

The time came when Jesus knew He would soon _______ for us. He rode a _________ into the city of _____________. Nobody else knew that _________ was going to _______. Many people came to _______________ Jesus as __________. They threw _______________ branches and __________ onto the road where He was coming. They shouted for _______________.

The people were right to think Jesus was _________. But He was not the kind of king they wanted. Jesus is King of ____________ as well as earth. He did not come to live in a palace and wear a crown. He came to be the Savior who would die for our sins and lead us to ______________.

Name:____________________

"I Am the Good Shepherd."

1. What does a shepherd do?

2. What would good sheep do?

3. Who is the Good Shepherd?

4. Who are His sheep?

Name:____________________

Complete this chart.

What a Shepherd Does	What Jesus Does
1. A shepherd knows his sheep.	
2. A shepherd watches over his sheep.	
3. A shepherd knows what his sheep want and need.	
4. A shepherd feeds his sheep.	
5. A shepherd protects his sheep.	
6. A shepherd looks for his lost sheep.	
7. A shepherd leads his sheep to green pastures.	
8. A shepherd cares for the injured sheep.	

Name: ____________________

Jesus Is the Way

Can you write what it means to be:

OBEDIENT: ______________________________

How can we be obedient? Give an example.

____

____

HUMBLE: ______________________________

How can we be humble? Give an example.

____

____

FORGIVING: ______________________________

How can we be forgiving? Give an example.

____

____

PRAYERFUL: ______________________________

How can we be prayerful? Give an example.

____

____

MERCIFUL: ______________________________

How can we be merciful? Give an example.

____

____

Name: ____________________

Jesus Is With Us Always.

He comes to live in us.

1. What is the Eucharist?

2. When did Jesus give us the Eucharist?

3. What is Transubstantiation?

4. Into what are the bread and wine changed?

Name:____________________

Before the Prayers of Consecration

What we offer to God is bread made of wheat, and wine made of grapes. These gifts become our spiritual food, the Body and Blood of Jesus. This change of "substance" or the "what it is" occurs at a moment called TRANSUBSTANTIATION.

TRANSUBSTANTIATION

After the Prayers of Consecration

No longer are bread and wine present, but Jesus! It is His Body, Blood, Soul and Divinity, really and truly present in the Blessed Sacrament. We receive Jesus in Holy Communion and He comes to bring us His life in our souls. Jesus is the Bread of Life.

Name:______________________

This is my Body, which will be given up for you. This is the chalice of my Blood...which will be poured out for you and for many for the forgiveness of sins.

Name:____________________

Jesus Is the Bread of Life

Fill in the blanks. Use textbook pages 107–8 for help.

The night before ___________ died, He celebrated the _______________ dinner with his twelve ____________. Jesus felt very ___________ to be leaving His friends. He wanted there to be a way that He could always _________ with them, and with all those who loved Him.

So, while they were eating, Jesus took some ________. He prayed to his Father, blessed the ____________, and broke it. He gave it to His disciples and said:

____

_________Then Jesus took a _______________ and said:

____

____

____

With those words, the ___________ and ___________ became the_________________and______________of Jesus. It was _________ bread and wine anymore, but _____________. When the disciples ate it, Jesus came to live in their ____________. This was the first time anyone had received ___________ ______________________.

Name:____________________

Answer the following questions.

1. Where did Jesus and His disciples go after the Last Supper?

2. Why was Jesus sad?

3. What did Jesus tell His Father?

4. What happened after Jesus was arrested?

Draw Jesus in the garden. Add yourself praying with Jesus.

Name:____________________

The Apostles' Creed

I believe in God, the Father almighty, Creator of heaven and earth, and in Jesus Christ, his only Son, our Lord, who was conceived by the Holy Spirit, born of the Virgin Mary, suffered under Pontius Pilate, was crucified, died, and was buried; he descended into hell; on the third day he rose again from the dead; he ascended into heaven, and is seated at the right hand of God the Father almighty; from there he will come to judge the living and the dead. I believe in the Holy Spirit, the holy catholic Church, the communion of saints, the forgiveness of sins, the resurrection of the body, and life everlasting. *Amen.*

You will have to study hard to learn this creed. Say it often and write it out. Ask Jesus to help you to learn this statement of our Holy Faith. Mark the days in which you say the Apostles' Creed this week.

Monday	Tuesday	Wednesday	Thursday	Friday	Saturday	Sunday

Name:______________________

We adore You, O Christ, and we bless You, because by Your Holy Cross, You have redeemed the world.

Name:____________________

Word Search

Can you find these words in the puzzle? Look carefully!

JESUS	SHEEP	WATCHES	BODY
KING	OBEDIENT	PROTECT	BREAD
SHEPHERD	HUMBLE	FEED	BLOOD
SACRAMENTS	FORGIVING	SON	WINE
LOVE	MERCIFUL	GARDEN	MEMORY

P	E	M	E	J	K	E	S	S	S	I	O
R	W	E	F	E	I	H	A	L	H	S	B
O	A	R	O	S	N	U	C	O	E	H	E
T	T	C	R	U	G	M	R	V	E	E	D
E	C	I	G	S	V	B	A	E	P	P	I
C	H	F	I	U	L	L	M	E	A	H	E
T	E	U	V	B	G	E	E	R	M	E	N
B	S	L	I	R	A	Y	N	A	E	R	T
L	W	H	N	E	R	B	T	I	M	D	F
O	I	B	G	A	D	O	S	R	O	S	E
O	N	O	O	D	E	D	E	D	R	O	E
D	E	R	R	O	N	Y	O	R	Y	N	D

Name:____________________

Jesus Christ Is Risen Today!

Write how you would feel if you went to the tomb and found it empty. Also write about meeting the angel and knowing that your Lord is Risen!

____

____

____

____

____

____

____

____

____

____

Name:____________________

Put these events in order:

PART I:

_____ Jesus taught us about loving God and our neighbor and worked many miracles.

_____ Jesus was baptized by John the Baptist.

_____ Jesus was born of the Virgin Mary in Bethlehem.

PART II

_____ Jesus carried a heavy Cross to Mount Calvary.

_____ Jesus forgave the good thief.

_____ Jesus rode into Jerusalem on a donkey.

_____ Jesus went to the Garden of Olives to pray.

_____ Jesus celebrated the Last Supper with His disciples and gave us the Eucharist.

_____ Jesus was nailed to the Cross.

_____ Jesus rose from the dead on Easter Sunday.

_____ Soldiers came to arrest Jesus.

Name:____________________

Our Lord is risen from the dead. He won for us eternal life! Jesus is true God and true man. He is a Divine Person who took on a human nature. We show this by the color of His clothes. Jesus often is shown wearing a blue robe (divinity) and a red coat (humanity). Can you color His clothes?

Name:____________________

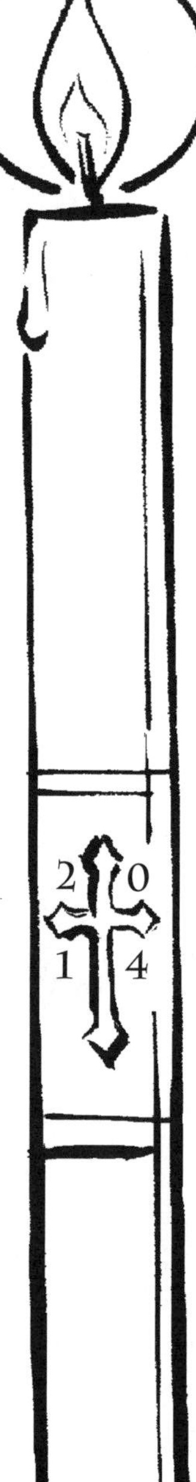

The Paschal Candle is lit on Easter Sunday. It is a white candle with special marks on it. Can you draw these marks?

1. There is a large red Cross on the candle (See page 118 in your textbook for a pattern).

2. At the top of the Cross is an "A", or in Greek this is called an alpha. It means the beginning.

3. At the bottom of the Cross is an upside down horseshoe. In Greek this is a letter called an omega. It means the end. The alpha and omega remind us that Jesus is the Beginning and the End—that He is the Eternal God.

4. Usually in the corners of the Cross, are the numbers of the date, e.g., for the year 2014 we would see:

20

+

14

The center and four points of the Cross are marked with cloves, reminding us of Christ's wounds.

Name:______________________

Sunday is God's Day

List ways to make the Lord's Day special.

____

____

____

____

____

____

____

____

____

Draw yourself honoring God on Sunday.

Name:____________________

Make a poster inviting people to Mass.

Name:____________________

Can you fill in the blanks?

Every _________ we go to _________ to do what _________ told us to do when He said, "Do this in _______________ of Me." You see, the __________ __________ was the very first ____________.

At the Last Supper, Jesus changed ___________ and __________ into His _______ and __________. He gave the ____________ the power to do this too. The ___________ gave that _____________ to other men. That is why our _____________ today can change ___________ and _______________ into the _________ and ___________ of Christ at every ________.

At Mass, we offer the same _________ that Jesus offered for our ________. That is the _________ which Jesus offered to the ___________ when He died on the _______. A sacrifice is the total giving up to God of something dear to us. Jesus gave _________ up for us to God the Father. This is the ___________ we offer at every Mass.

Name:____________________

Word Search

Can you find these words in the puzzle?
Look carefully! The words go across and down.

BREAD	SACRIFICE	GRACE	CHURCH
COMMUNITY	SUNDAY	POWER	DISCIPLES
EASTER	BLOOD	PRIEST	CAREFULLY
OFFERED	CELEBRATE	SINS	RESURRECTION
PRAY	CROSS	BODY	WINE

R	E	S	U	R	R	E	C	T	I	O	N
S	O	F	F	E	R	E	D	W	D	S	B
A	B	C	R	O	S	S	C	I	I	C	O
C	L	P	R	I	E	S	T	N	S	A	D
R	O	P	O	W	E	R	A	E	C	R	Y
I	O	B	R	E	A	D	M	E	I	E	E
F	D	C	H	U	R	C	H	R	P	F	A
I	S	L	I	G	R	A	C	E	L	U	S
C	E	L	E	B	R	A	T	E	E	L	T
E	I	B	G	A	D	S	I	N	S	L	E
S	U	N	D	A	Y	D	P	R	A	Y	R
D	E	R	C	O	M	M	U	N	I	T	Y

Name:____________________

Word Search

Can you find these words in the puzzle?
Look carefully! The words go across and down.

ALTAR	CHALICE	ENTRANCE
BIBLE	CIBORIUM	FORGIVE
BLESSED	COMMUNION	JESUS
BLOOD	CREED	BODY
	CRUETS	

A L T A R B L E S S E D
C O M M U N I O N D C B
A E F O R G I V E C R I
C N P R I E S T N O E B
C T P O W E R A E N E L
I R B R E A D M E F D E
B A C H U R C H R S F B
O N L I G J E S U S U L
R C L E B C R U E T S O
I E B G A D S I N S L O
U U N D A Y D P R A Y D
M C H A L I C E B O D Y

Name: ____________________

This Year We Receive Our First Communion!

Color the picture.

Name:____________________

INSTRUMENT	WHAT IT IS	DRAW IT
Altar		
Chalice		
Ciborium		
Cruets		
Missal		
Paten		
Tabernacle		
Monstrance		

Name:____________________

Parts of Mass	What the Priest Does	What We Do
Entrance:		
Readings:		
Offertory:		
Consecration:		
Communion:		
Blessing:		

Name:____________________

The Words of the Mass

Use your crayons to underline words from this prayer of the Mass. Follow these instructions:

- With a red crayon, underline the words that the priest says to consecrate the bread.
- With a brown crayon, underline the words that the priest says to consecrate the wine.
- With a blue crayon, underline the words calling on the Holy Spirit.
- With an orange crayon, underline the words that tell why Jesus died for us.

"You are indeed Holy, O Lord, the fount of all holiness. Make holy, therefore, these gifts, we pray, by sending down your Spirit upon them like the dewfall, so that they may become for us the Body and Blood of our Lord, Jesus Christ.

At the time he was betrayed and entered willingly into his Passion, he took bread and, giving thanks, broke it, and gave it to his disciples, saying:

> Take this, all of you, and eat of it, for this is my Body, which will be given up for you.

In a similar way, when supper was ended, he took the chalice and, once more giving thanks, he gave it to his disciples, saying:

> Take this, all of you, and drink from it, for this is the chalice of my Blood, the Blood of the new and eternal covenant, which will be poured out for you and for many for the forgiveness of sins. Do this in memory of me."

Name:____________________

Draw a picture of yourself spending time with Jesus after having received Him in the Holy Eucharist.

When you receive First _______ ______________, it will be one of the ______________ things that ever happens to you. At ______________ you received a share in God's life. When you receive ________ ________________, you will have even ______ of God's ______. ___________, Himself, will be with you.

Just as food makes our bodies ______________, Holy Communion makes our __________ strong and beautiful. Jesus will be __________ to you than ever before. He will ____________ to everything you tell Him.

Name:____________________

Ask someone about his first Holy Communion. Explain to him why you are doing this, and ask his permission first.

1. Whom am I interviewing?

____

2. When did you receive your first Holy Communion?

____

3. Please tell me about that special day.

____

4. What did you wear?

____

5. Who was there with you?

____

6. Who said the Mass? At what Church?

____

7. Do you remember what you were thinking/praying?

____

8. Other comments you have:

____

Name:______________________

My Lord and My God!

Color the picture.

Name:____________________

Write a letter to Jesus inviting Him into your soul.

Dear Jesus,

____

____

____

____

____

____

____

____

____

____

Love,

____

This page intentionally left blank.

Name:____________________

Write a prayer to Jesus in the Blessed Sacrament.

Dear Jesus,

____

____

____

____

____

____

____

____

____

____

Love,

____

Name:____________________

The steps to receiving the Blessed Sacrament worthily.

STEP 3
We must consider Whom we are about to receive. Pay attention at Mass and say the responses. Pray to Jesus. Show in your daily life that you love Jesus by your words and actions. Tell Jesus you know He is present in the Eucharist and want to receive Him.

STEP 2
We must fast for one hour before receiving Holy Communion. We may not eat or drink anything except water before Communion. (We may drink water and take medicine if we need to before Communion.) It is good to prepare to receive Jesus.

STEP 1
Make sure your soul is healthy. We may never receive Communion if we have mortal sins on our souls. Examine your conscience and go to the Sacrament of Penance first if you need to. It is good to confess venial sins, too.

Name:____________________

What can you pray before you receive Holy Communion?

____

____

____

____

What can you pray after you receive Holy Communion?

____

____

____

____

Name: ____________________

Receiving Jesus

Fill in the blanks with the words below to complete the sentences.

one	respect	listening	thank	healthy

We Receive Jesus:

1. First I will ask myself if my soul is _____________.
2. I will make sure I do not eat or drink anything ______ hour before I receive Holy Communion.
3. I get ready for Jesus by __________________ and praying during Mass.
4. I receive Jesus in Holy Communion with love and _________________________.
5. When I get back to my seat I will ______________ Jesus for coming to me.

Name:____________________

The Apostles

Draw a picture of Jesus sending His Apostles.

After He rose from the dead, Jesus stayed on earth for forty days. He appeared to His disciples many times. He gave the Apostles the power to forgive sins. He told them how to bring the Good News to places all over the world. An Apostle is one "who is sent." Jesus was sending them to teach all people about His saving love.

Name:____________________

It is the Lord!

One day, the Apostles were out in a boat, fishing. They could not find many fish. A voice from the shore called, "Cast the net on the right side." It was Jesus, but they did not know it. They did what He said and pulled up so many fish that they could not lift the net.

Then, John, the Beloved Disciple, knew Who was on the shore. "It is the Lord," he shouted. Peter was so excited that he jumped into the water and swam to the beach.

What would you do if you knew Jesus was close by?

____

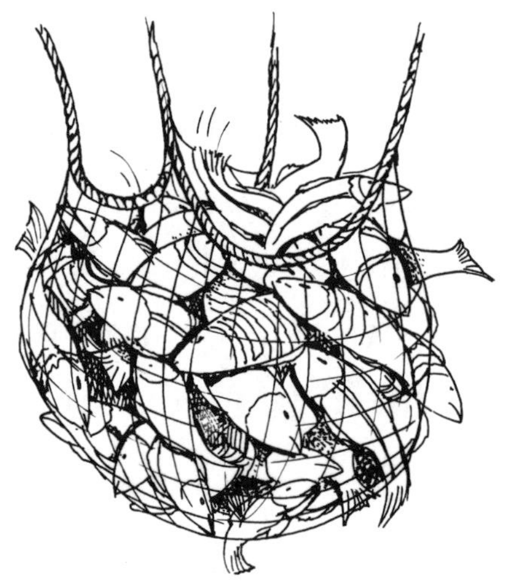

Name:______________________

Do you love me?

Draw Peter swimming to meet Jesus on the shore.

You know that I love you.

Name:____________________

Color the picture of Jesus' Ascension.

As the Apostles watched, Jesus rose up into the sky and went back to Heaven. There He is King of Heaven and earth. He has prepared a place in Heaven for all who are faithful to Him. He is at the right hand of the Father. With the Father, He sent the Holy Spirit.

Name:______________________

Pentecost

Color the picture of Pentecost.

Name:____________________

Word Search

Can you find these words in the puzzle?
Look carefully! The words go across and down.

APOSTLE	THIRD PERSON	MARY
BAPTIZED	FIRE	PRAYED
HOLY SPIRIT	GIFTS	TEACH
PENTECOST	JESUS	TRINITY
PREACH		WIN

B	A	P	T	I	Z	E	D	W	I	N	P
S	T	H	I	R	D	P	E	R	S	O	N
A	P	R	E	A	C	H	C	I	S	T	P
C	J	M	A	R	Y	R	T	N	C	R	E
R	E	P	R	A	Y	E	D	T	A	I	N
I	S	B	R	E	A	D	M	E	P	N	T
O	U	M	H	U	R	C	H	R	L	I	E
I	S	L	I	G	R	A	C	E	E	T	C
T	E	A	C	H	G	I	F	T	S	Y	O
E	I	G	I	F	T	S	F	I	R	E	S
H	O	L	Y	S	P	I	R	I	T	L	T
D	E	R	C	O	A	P	O	S	T	L	E

Name:____________________

Holy Spirit

The Holy Spirit, Who came to the Apostles, is the Third Person of the Blessed Trinity. The Holy Spirit came to us at Baptism. He helps us to pray and to love. He gives us the grace to win the fight against sin. He helps us to understand the things we learn about God. He will come to us in a special way when we are confirmed.

Color the picture.

Name:____________________

What Are Sacraments?

SACRAMENT	EXPLAIN THIS SACRAMENT
BAPTISM	
PENANCE	
HOLY EUCHARIST	
CONFIRMATION	
MARRIAGE	
HOLY ORDERS	
ANOINTING OF THE SICK	

Name:____________________

Apostles' Creed

Can you fill in the blanks?

I __________ in God, the __________ __________, __________ of heaven and earth, and in __________ __________, his only _____, our Lord, who was _____________ by the _________ _________, born of the __________ _________, suffered under ___________ ____________, was __________, died, and was buried; he descended into _______; on the _________ day he rose again from the dead; he ascended into _________, and is seated at the ________ hand of God the ____________ almighty; from there he will come to ___________ the __________ and the __________. I __________ in the __________ ____________, the holy __________ Church, the ________________ of saints, the forgiveness of ______, the _______________________ of the body, and life _________________. *Amen.*

Name:____________________

Answer the following questions.

1. Who did Jesus make as head of His Church?

2. Who has Peter's job now? What is His name?

3. What do bishops do?

4. What do the Pope and the bishops together do?

5. What do priests do?

6 What do deacons do?

7. What do religious brothers and sisters do?

8. The rest of us are called laity. What do we do?

Name:______________________

God's Family

______________________ ______________________

______________________ ______________________

Can you label each of these pictures?

Priest Pope Bishop Laity

Name:____________________

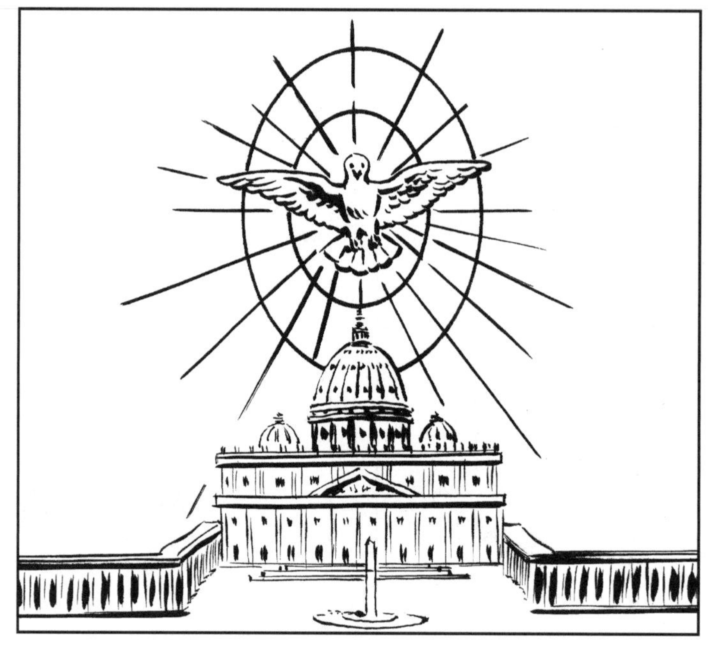

The Church is like a ________. It has many ________. If even one small part is hurt or missing, the whole __________ suffers. Each small part does something that others cannot do. ______ can help the __________ in a way that ____ _____ else can. And the _________ and __________ of many others help you.

The Church makes us _______. It brings the ________ of God to everyone. Each of us can ____________ that grace and become ______. We can also bring ________'s _______ and ________ to others.

Name:____________________

Assumption

Color the picture.

Mary was taken to Heaven with her body and soul.

Name:____________________

Color the picture.

Just as the Child Jesus could go to Mary, so can we go to our Mother. We can ask her to pray for us, to help us, and to bring us closer to her Son, Jesus. Mary loves us all.

Name:____________________

Color the picture.

Mary is a most beautiful and wonderful person.

Name:____________________

Answer the following questions.

1. Where was Mary at Pentecost?

2. Did Mary help the Church to grow?

3. Why is Mary the Mother of the Church?

4. What did God do for Mary that was so special?

5. Of what is Mary Queen?

6. Did Mary ever sin?

7. How can Mary help us to be good and pleasing to God?

8. For whom does Mary have a special love? How do we know this?

9. What prayer did Mary ask for people to pray?

Name:____________________

Answer the following questions.

1. How is Jesus with us?

2. What is the special way that Jesus is with us?

3. What is in the tabernacle?

4. How can you tell Jesus is present in the church?

5. Is Jesus really in the church?

Draw a beautiful tabernacle for Jesus.

Name:____________________

List some times you can stop into the church to visit Jesus.

____
____
____
____
____
____
____
____
____
____

Write a poem about Jesus in the Blessed Sacrament.

____
____
____
____
____
____
____
____
____

Name:______________________

Draw a monstrance on the altar. Put a candle on each side to show that Christ is present.

Name:____________________

Draw people, angels, and saints worshiping our Lord in the Eucharist.

Name:____________________

Word Search

Can you find these words in the puzzle?
Look carefully! The words go across and down.

BODIES	REUNITED	GOD	MARY
HEAVEN	DIE	VENIAL SIN	SOULS
MORTAL SIN	HELL	HOME	PURGATORY

M	O	R	T	A	L	S	I	N	D	I	E
R	G	O	D	E	R	E	D	W	D	S	H
E	B	P	U	R	G	A	T	O	R	Y	E
U	L	H	O	M	E	S	T	N	S	A	L
N	F	O	R	A	V	E	R	E	C	R	L
I	O	B	R	R	A	D	M	E	I	E	E
T	D	C	H	Y	R	C	H	R	P	F	A
E	S	T	R	I	N	I	Y	E	L	U	S
D	E	L	E	B	R	A	T	E	E	L	T
E	I	B	V	E	N	I	A	L	S	I	N
S	O	U	L	S	Y	H	E	A	V	E	N
D	E	R	B	O	D	I	E	S	I	T	Y

Name:______________________

Draw a picture of you in your true home, Heaven.

Name:____________________

Color the squares that will help you get to Heaven in red. Color the squares that will not help you get to Heaven in blue.

Hide a letter to your parents	Hit your brother or sister	Not include a friend in your games
Play with your brother or sister	Visit Jesus at church	Pick on a student at school
Talk back to your father	Say God's name in vain	Watch TV during prayer
Disobey your mother	Decide to play and not pray	Visit your grandmother
Help your mom at home	Pray for your sick friend	Do not learn your answers for school
Learn your prayers	Be nice to everyone	Say bad words
Study for your test	Say something mean	Feed the dog
Tell a lie	Do your homework	Play rough at recess
Talk during Mass	Pick up your toys	Tell the truth

Name:____________________

Answer the following questions.

1. Who is in Heaven?

2. How can we get to Heaven?

3. Do all people go to Heaven? Where might they go?

4. Who goes to Purgatory? What happens there?

5. Who goes to Hell? What happens there?

6. What will happen at the end of the world?

7. Why are we on earth?

8. Where is our true home?

9. What is the most beautiful sight?